IN THE REAL

In the Realms of Gold

The Story of the Carnegie Medal

KEITH BARKER

*Much have I travell'd in the realms of gold,
And many goodly states and kingdoms seen.*

KEATS
On first looking into Chapman's Homer

Julia MacRae Books

IN ASSOCIATION WITH THE YOUTH LIBRARIES GROUP
OF THE LIBRARY ASSOCIATION

Copyright © 1986 Keith Barker
All rights reserved
First published in Great Britain in 1986
by Julia MacRae Books,
A division of Franklin Watts,
12a Golden Square, London W1R 4BA
and Franklin Watts Australia,
14 Mars Road, Lane Cove, NSW 2066
Published in association with
the Youth Libraries Group of The Library Association

Typeset by Cambrian Typesetters Frimley, Surrey
Printed in Great Britain by A Wheaton & Co. Ltd, Exeter

British Library Cataloguing in Publication Data
Barker, Keith
In the realms of the gold: the story of
the Carnegie Medal.
1. Library Association Carnegie Medal
I. Title
809'.89282'079   PR990
ISBN 0–86203–260–1

TO LIZ, WAVENEY AND ALWENA

Contents

Acknowledgements, ix

Introduction, 1

1
Chosen by adults for children, 3

2
'The Great Unread': The Carnegie Books, 17

3
Getting the Carnegie Medal Publicised, 31

Conclusion, 39

Bibliography, 44

APPENDIX A
Chronological history of the Carnegie Medal, 50

APPENDIX B
Carnegie Medal winners and Commended books, 1936–1984, 52

Index, 59

Acknowledgements

The research for this book was originally carried out for a Master's thesis at the College of Librarianship, Wales, and I am grateful to Frank Keyse for his expert supervision. I would like to acknowledge the Library Association for permitting access to council and committee minutes and the Youth Libraries Group, particularly Grace Shaw, for access to its minutes. John Dunne, Liam Parker and the YLG very kindly allowed me to observe the 1984 medal selection meetings. I would like also to thank The Bodley Head for permission to include an extract from *Memory in a House* by Lucy Boston, (1973); and Oxford University Press for permission to include the verse on p. 21.

Sheila Ray and Margaret Marshall Macdonald gave helpful advice at the outset of this project and Vivien Griffiths has expertly kept me on the correct path. My good friend John Visser made a number of valuable suggestions and Mary Green has displayed her usual skill at typing the manuscript. The book is dedicated to my wife and two daughters, all of whom display a healthy mistrust for any Carnegie Medal book.

Introduction

This book has been written with the general reader in mind. I discovered when I started to write that the subject tended to get grouped into three areas which became the basis for the three chapters. These in fact seek to answer three questions: one, who selects the Carnegie Medal; two, what sort of books are honoured; and three, how is the award publicised and promoted? Where applicable, the relevant parts of the history of the medal are included in the attempt to answer these questions. I intend that the tone of the book will be celebratory but not uncritical.

In writing the book, I have been forced to consider why the Carnegie Medal is so important. It is important because it is the oldest of the British children's book awards and because it has received far more criticism (much of this unjust) than any of the other awards. Its history should therefore teach some lessons. I do not see it doing this, for some of the mistakes made are being repeated with other awards, both new and established. It is important because it is still capable of generating controversy: I feel that the day an award inspires complacency is the day it should be laid to rest. And finally it is important because it has shown that a group of professionals not widely regarded for their critical acumen can still honour as many good and as many duff books as the critics and authors who make up other selection committees.

Let us hope it continues to do so.

1
Chosen by adults for children

Before the baby is christened, it is important to discover its conception and birth.

The Carnegie Medal is named after Andrew Carnegie, the Scottish-born philanthropist who provided the funding for many British public libraries. 1935 was the centenary of Carnegie's birth and it was decided that a medal should be instituted in celebration of this. The medal would honour a particular form of literature and it would be presented annually by the Library Association. But what particular aspect of literature should be chosen? This was left to a sub-committee of the Association's executive committee to decide. One man who had suggested as early as 1931 that an award should be made for children's literature was W. C. Berwick Sayers, chief librarian of Croydon. This was also a matter of some national pride, for the American Library Association had instituted its own medal, the Newbery Medal, as far back as 1922. It was not surprising, therefore, that this sub-committee should recommend that children's literature be the field which would be recognised by the Carnegie Medal and on 2nd April, 1936, the Library Association executive committee accepted the recommendation that 'a gold medal be made annually for the best children's book published during the year by a British author'.

Having decided on the principle of the exercise, it was then necessary to work out the practicalities of making an annual award. This is often an area where organisers of awards find themselves in difficulties. It is comparatively easy to announce that an award will be made but not so easy to devise criteria for decision-making, or methods of applying these criteria. The Library Association instituted a method which at the time must have seemed foolproof but which time showed to have had many pitfalls. There would be a selection committee consisting of four dignitaries of the Library Association, the editor of *Library Association Record* (the Association's professional journal), the editor of *Library Assistant*, the chairman of the executive committee and the chairman of the council. The method of selection was to be that invitations would be sent out to the chief librarians of 'many important libraries' (just how many these many important libraries were was never actually specified, however). These chief librarians, in consultation with their children's librarians, would be allowed to submit up to six titles placed in order of merit. These would then be pooled and a winner would be found.

Although this plan sounds incredibly simple, and indeed similar schemes have been suggested throughout the medal's history, what was to be the role of the selection committee in all this? The method of selection implies that its role would be purely administrative and that it would merely gather together the submissions from the many important libraries and then count them. But would four important personages of the Library Association accept this passive role? Evidence suggests not. The first Carnegie Medal winner was announced in *Library Association Record* by W. C. Berwick Sayers, architect of the medal and a member of the selection committee until 1952. The winner of the first Carnegie Medal was Arthur Ransome's *Pigeon Post*. There was also a second and third prize winner in a manner similar to that used in modern beauty contests. In his announcement, Sayers states quite explicitly that the reason these books did not win the award was because the second prize winner, Howard Spring's *Sampson's Circus*, and the third prize winner, Noel Streatfeild's *Ballet Shoes*, appealed to only one group of children whereas *Pigeon Post* was of appeal to both boys and girls. This implies that the selection committee did slightly more than add up the votes from the many important libraries.

So what happened to change this situation where a small

number of librarians, none of whom was working with children, was making the selection, to the present method whereby a committee of thirteen people, all of whom are working with children in some capacity, choose from a list submitted by the library profession after consultation with other interested groups such as parents, teachers and often children?

One way this has been achieved is through the gradual wresting away of the influence of the Library Association. This was important, particularly in the early years of the Carnegie Medal, because the Library Association, having introduced the award, showed a lamentable lack of interest in promoting it. It failed to announce the medal winners for the first two years after the introduction of the medal. The members of the selection committee failed to attend selection meetings: only two members were present at the meeting where Noel Streatfeild's *The Circus is Coming* was chosen. The situation became so bad that in 1944 Eleanor Graham was complaining that 'the whole affair has, indeed, taken on a dangerously parochial air, as though it were the private and domestic concern of the Library Association'.

One person who was prepared to tackle the parochialism of the Library Association was Eileen Colwell, children's librarian at Hendon. She and Ethel Hayler had founded the Association of Children's Librarians in 1937 with the encouragement of W. C. Berwick Sayers (Ethel Hayler was, indeed, Sayers's children's librarian). However, the Library Association regarded this group as, in Robert Leeson's words, 'a sort of Communist plot' and refused to let it become affiliated to the main professional body of British librarians. The Association of Children's Librarians was particularly incensed about *The Circus is Coming* débâcle and put pressure to bear on the selection committee to allow a representative from the group to sit on that committee. When this was allowed in 1940, the voice of children's librarians began to be heard in debates about prize-winning children's literature. Eileen Colwell was a member of the committee that year and every subsequent year until 1968. Her presence began to have an effect, even though some of her efforts were thwarted by officialdom. When the selection committee suggested that no award be made in 1940, it was immediately told by the executive committee that Eleanor Doorly's *The Radium Woman* would be the Carnegie Medal winner for that year. When the selection committee suggested that the medal would be better chosen by the membership at large, it was informed that selection by committee would continue.

Nevertheless Eileen Colwell did manage to chip into some of the barriers of the Library Association. The term 'an outstanding book for children' replaced 'best book for children' (a dangerous expression and one used by few of the British children's book awards). Written criteria were also used for the first time during the war period. Admittedly these criteria were not extensive in scope but they were an improvement on the vagueness which had surrounded previous decisions of the selection committee.

What Eileen Colwell and her companions on the Association of Children's Librarians really wanted, however, was a selection committee which consisted primarily of children's librarians. This was one of the suggestions made by the group in 1942 but it was to be another twenty-six years before this apparently radical suggestion was carried out. Some success was achieved when the Association of Children's Librarians in 1947 became the 'Youth Libraries Section', an affiliated group to the Library Association. It may well be that this move gave the group some sort of respectability, for within two years of its formation the Youth Libraries Section had secured for itself an equal representation on the selection committee. And with that the Youth Libraries Section (still under the aegis of Eileen Colwell) appeared to be content, for there was very little pressure, either from within or outside the selection committee, to alter the situation until the turbulent events of the late 1960s.

This period of inactivity may have seemed to confer an air of tranquillity on the structure of the Carnegie Medal selection committee: it did also mean that members of this committee tended to be long-stay rather than short-stay. The selection committee individual members were virtually the same from the late 1940s until well into the 1950s. This longevity in membership was particularly evident in the case of those representatives of the publications committee, the group which just after the war was given responsibility for the selection of the medal. Bruce Stevenson, a representative of the publications committee, was a member of the selection committee for over twenty years, Lorna Paulin for over fifteen, and E. V. Corbett for ten years. This is in direct contrast with the situation when the committee structure was changed in 1969 where eight out of ten of the new committee members were sitting on the selection committee for the first time. In 1984, when I attended the selection meetings as an observer, one of the thirteen members had been on the committee twice before, four had been members once previously, and the remaining eight were all sitting on the panel for the first time.

There are, of course, advantages to both systems mentioned above. The long term method of selection does mean that there is a tradition of book selection developed, and this can be seen in the Carnegie Medal winners of the post-war period. However, this system does also mean that the same type of book tends to be honoured: one of the motives for changing the committee structure in the 1960s was that one publishing house, Oxford University Press, was continually winning the prizes. It may well depend on the attitude of mind of the selectors, for a number of the members of the selection panel for The Other Award have been on that panel for ten years and there is no way that particular award or the books it selects can be described as fossilised.

One reason for changing the members of the selection committee for the Carnegie Medal, particularly today, is the large number of librarians who want to sit on that committee. This started to become a problem during the 1960s and was one of the contributory factors to the turbulence which surrounded the Carnegie Medal in this period, which was eventually to force the Library Association to alter the committee structure. The sixties are regarded in retrospect as a period of expansion in children's librarianship. Between 1954 and 1962, for instance, the number of specialist children's posts had risen by over twelve per cent. Some county libraries, such as West Riding and

Kent, and boroughs like Luton and Sunderland, had established separate children's libraries. The Library Association had instituted papers in its examinations on library work with children, and on children's literature. In addition, increased attention was paid to the criticism of children's books. Pioneers in this field included Margaret Meek, E. W. Hildick, Margery Fisher and Naomi Lewis, while Brian Alderson, children's book editor of *The Times*, became the Carnegie Medal's sternest critic. A monk called Brother Aidan began to publish critical pieces on children's literature and later, as Aidan Chambers, he launched a sustained attack on the medal in his book *The Reluctant Reader*.

All of these developments were bound to have an effect on attitudes towards children's books and it was inevitable that the administrators of the Carnegie Medal would have to make changes to the award as, indeed, all awards should be amended periodically if they are to retain any credibility. Pressure for change came first from the selection committee and then from regional branches of the Youth Libraries Group (all Library Association sections were reclassified as groups in 1962). But it was not until the debate was opened out into the correspondence pages of *The Times Literary Supplement* that the Library Association made any significant concessions.

The steps towards change began in 1966 when Eileen Colwell and her colleagues on the selection committee again asked for the Youth Libraries Group to be allowed to take total responsibility for the selection of the medal. (Having asked this for three different groups, the YLG, the YLS and the Association of Children's Librarians, Eileen Colwell must surely have been experiencing a feeling of *déjà vu*.) The publications committee yet again dismissed this idea but conceded that the YLG should be the body to make the preliminary selection of the list of suggestions and then forward a list of between six and twelve titles, together with detailed comments, to the final selection committee. However, as one librarian noted in a letter to the professional journal, the selection committee still reserved the right to make the final decision, possibly against the advice of the YLG 'who are expected to give time and experience to assessing the short listed books, but without the ultimate responsibility for the award itself'. Nevertheless, the YLG agreed to submit a short list of up to five titles, probably believing that half a loaf was better than no bread.

Children's librarians continued to make suggestions for change from 1965. The most vociferous of the medal's critics were the Surrey children's librarians group and the London and Home Counties branch of the Youth Libraries Group, represented by a young Lambeth librarian, Janet Hill. Janet Hill's doubts about the medal were further strengthened when she joined the selection committee in 1967. She found that she was only given seven days to examine the list of twenty-seven potential titles for the Carnegie Medal. The YLG selection committee which she joined contained only children's librarians who were in supervisory positions in libraries, as indeed she was herself. The first selection meeting, she felt, was 'surprisingly brief', and the final meeting of the selection committee was attended by only two of the four representatives of the publications committee.

The whole process obviously left Janet Hill with a feeling of dismay and she was determined to try to change the system. Her presence on the committee may have had some effect on the decision to withhold the Carnegie Medal for that year, the only occasion in peacetime when the selection committee has felt it important to undertake a relatively drastic step. It was not a popular decision: the American Janice Dohm, writing anonymously as 'A Librarian' in *Junior Bookshelf*, described it as 'a poor thin way of doing things' and claimed it had 'left everyone concerned feeling rueful and ruffled and looking distinctly shabby'. It was perhaps unfortunate that this was the last year in which Eileen Colwell sat on the selection committee. Perhaps, though, she would have wished to bow out in this way: she did, after all, make efforts to have the Carnegie Medal withheld in the very first year she was a member of the committee, a decision which the Library Association overturned.

In 1967 the Youth Libraries Group selection committee suggested to the Library Association that another medal be introduced which would be similar to America's Laura Ingalls Wilder Award and would be made for the corpus of an author's work. The suggested title for this medal was to be the Colwell Medal. It is unfortunate that the library profession has not yet seen fit to introduce such an award, for it would certainly fill an unnecessary gap in British children's book awards and could be used to honour authors who have produced work of a consistently high standard but have never received the accolade of the Carnegie Medal. Others may like to suggest their own names, but children's writers from the past and present who have not been honoured include Alison Uttley, Joan Aiken, Nina Bawden and John Rowe Townsend.

It is highly probable that Eileen Colwell, Colwell Medal or not, was gratified that children's librarians were making strenuous efforts to change the terms of the Carnegie Medal. The fact that this meant she was dislodged from the selection committee would have been a small price to pay. Discussions about the award occupied a great deal of time at the Youth Libraries Group's annual weekend conference in 1967. Main areas for criticism included the constitution of the selection committee and the possibility of instituting a separate medal for non-fiction. There was also concern that the terms were not clear about authors being able to receive the Carnegie Medal more than once. The following year, when Peggy Heeks announced that the terms were being rewritten to make this more obvious, she said that authors had always been able to win the medal again. However, many had been confused by Marcus Crouch's definition in his book *Chosen for Children*, the official Carnegie Medal history. Some authors, such as William Mayne, Alan Garner and Rosemary Sutcliff, were quick to declare that they would refuse a second Carnegie Medal if they were offered one. In fact, it was only in 1980 that the Carnegie Medal was awarded to an author who had won one before, but of the five winning authors of the 1980s four of them, Peter Dickinson, Robert Westall, Jan Mark and Margaret Mahy, have been previous winners. Does this denote a lack of imagination on the part of successive selection committees or a limited number of top class children's writers during this decade?

Chosen by adults for children

Despite the demands for change which came both from the selection committee and from the library profession as a whole, it was not until the debate burst into the pages of *The Times Literary Supplement* that the Library Association announced any changes to the selection procedure. Ironically, this was in 1968, a year which contained the best list of winning books for some time: the medal winner was Alan Garner's *The Owl Service*, highly commended was Henry Treece's posthumously published novel, *The Dream Time*, and commended were Helen Cresswell's *The Piemakers*, Leon Garfield's *Smith*, and K. M. Peyton's *Flambards*. *The Times Literary Supplement* episode began with an article by Peggy Heeks, YLG chairman, in which she discussed how that year's selection committee had chosen *The Owl Service* (also the winner of the *Guardian* Award, introduced in 1966). Peggy Heeks declared the selection committee was not looking for 'the most popular book, the most promising book, the most socially useful book'; the Library Association, she believed, was recognising 'quality and quality full-grown, not in the bud.' This article provoked an attack from Brian Alderson, himself the winner of an award that year, the Children's Book Circle's Eleanor Farjeon Award. Criticising Peggy Heeks's apparent refusal to define more precisely the qualifications of the selection committee, and the Library Association's 'primitive' approach to publicity, Alderson asked for 'an intelligent critical account of the chief books considered together with an elucidation of the reasons for selecting the winners.'

Replying to these criticisms, Peggy Heeks said that it was 'heartening' to see interest in the Library Association medals from someone who was '. . . not a member. Librarians are seemingly less energetic.' She rebuked Brian Alderson for attending the annual general meeting of the YLG when the whole situation was discussed, again because he was 'not a member'.

Alderson found an ally, however, in Janet Hill, who wrote in support, reiterating her experiences as a member of the selection committee the previous year. It was at this point that Library Association ranks began to close. First of all, Bruce Stevenson, a member of the selection committee since 1946, wrote to say that by the time the committee met, all the members had read all of the books on the list and many had gauged 'the reactions of their child readers to the books.' The majority of the committee's decisions had been unanimous, he declared. The crowning touch to the whole affair came from E. V. Corbett, chairman of the publications committee, who closed the correspondence by demonstrating that the Library Association was not resistant to change. The following year, the Youth Libraries Group would be 'virtually responsible' for the recommendations to the council, subject only to the approval of the publications committee. (This particular restriction was to be lifted two years later). The terms of the award were also altered to make it possible for a non-British author to win the medal, as long as the winning book was first published in the United Kingdom.

Having achieved this sanction from the Library Association, the YLG selection committee, aided by the ubiquitous Janet Hill, now had the job of working out the practicalities. They decided the Carnegie Medal selection committee should consist of ten members, not necessarily limited to members of the YLG. The Chairman, Vice-Chairman and Honorary Secretary of the YLG would be ex-officio members of the selection committee and the remaining seven should include some who had everyday contact with children. This is the pattern which, with some modifications, is still in force.

This arrangement continued until the end of 1973 when the YLG national committee decided that the branches of the Youth Libraries Group should be invited to send representatives to the Carnegie Medal selection committee in order to involve the membership at large. This meant that the numbers on the committee were increased to eleven plus two ex-officio officers. There was some feeling that when this system had been in operation for some years, representatives might feel too restricted by the decisions of their branches, but it was felt that, rather like members of parliament, they would have to express their own views rather than attempt to represent a disparate group of views.

The involvement of branches was a deliberate attempt to

Chosen by adults for children

involve the membership at large in the selection of the award. A working party set up by the Library Association had in 1978 agreed that this was to be the aim, and modern selection committees have taken positive steps to reduce the secrecy which has surrounded the selection of the Carnegie Medal in the past. For it should be remembered that both the Carnegie Medal and the Library Association's other children's book award, the Kate Greenaway Medal, given for illustration, are unique among British children's book awards in that any one of the several thousand children's books published each year can be recommended by any member of the Library Association. Other awards are restricted to those books which publishers choose to nominate. This very openness has sometimes caused distress to those on the selection committee, and recommendations have been made, in 1978 by a working party set up by the Library Association and in 1982 by various past chairmen of the YLG committee, that some restriction be made on nominations, possibly by some type of points system. The method that is currently in use is to divide the initial list into three sections based on the number of votes each book has received. The selection committee is expected to have read all of the books in the first section (those with the most votes) and as many as possible from those in the other two sections. In 1984 there were forty-one books on the initial list (plus, of course, those nominated for the Kate Greenaway Medal, which in the same year were twenty-nine). Eight of these titles were in the first section, nine were in the second and twenty-four in the third. The selection committee receives the list at the beginning of March and by the middle of April is expected not only to have obtained these books (for the Library Association medals are not reliant on publishers' submissions) but also to have read as many of them as possible.

This may sound an incredibly daunting experience, but in fact there are always books on the initial list which have been potential winners throughout the year, and children's librarians in touch with developments in children's literature (which members of the selection committee are expected to be) will no doubt have already encountered them. For instance, on the 1984 list there were the *Guardian* Award winner, one of the Other Award winners and the winner of the Federation of Children's Book Groups award. However, there are always some surprise items: in 1984 a play published by a private press, and constantly over the years a number of Mabel Esther Allen's works. Every book on the 1984 list had been read by at least one member of the selection committee, a vast improvement on the situation in 1949 when the Youth Libraries Section asked that every member of the committee should be 'prepared' to read all of the recommended books on the final list, a list of six titles at the time.

Since 1976 it has been possible to include a book in English which has either had a simultaneous publication in another country or has been published elsewhere within three months of its U.K. publication. This may mean that members of the selection committee have spent time finding and reading a book which later proves ineligible for the Carnegie Medal. However, this does not apply to the majority of books for, of the forty-one books on the 1984 list, only one was by an American and two were by Australian writers.

The actual meetings of the selection committee take place on two separate days with a gap of a month between them. An experiment was tried in 1982 of having the selection meetings on consecutive days, but the committee discovered that this did not allow the time necessary for re-reading and carefully considering the books on the short list. It was obvious in 1984, for example, that the books on the short list would have been in a very different order from that in which they finally found themselves if the panel had not had good time to go away and consider them more carefully. Panel members have also been able to consult their colleagues in recent years, for the short list has been publicly announced. There was, of course, a sound reason for holding the selection meetings on consecutive days: cost. In late 1981, the Library Association was finding itself in a severe financial crisis and was looking for alternative ways to administer its medal procedure, possibly with the help of an outside body like the National Book League (which now, of course, administers another children's book award, sponsored by a sweets firm). Rather than let this happen, and until a trust fund could be set up to pay for the awards, the YLG agreed to take the financial responsibility for the administration of the medals. One obvious way to cut down the cost of the medals procedure was to have to pay only one set of fares to the selection committee members. In early 1982, for instance, of the £1,500 spent on the administration of the medals, £1,000 was spent on panel meetings. Nonetheless, after trying the plan of consecutive meetings once, the YLG committee decided that the aesthetic disadvantages far outweighed the financial advantages. It is indeed comforting to know that the YLG is prepared to put the worth of the Carnegie Medal before Mammon.

The nominations which finally reach the selection committee come from three groups: from individual members of the Library Association; from the eleven YLG branches which generally hold meetings at the beginning of each year and can, like the other two groups, nominate up to three titles; and from local authority libraries. This third group made the most significant number of suggestions to the 1984 list (58% of the total). Indeed, if it had not been for a nomination from a local authority, one of the four books on the short list would not have been considered. Local authorities vary in the arrangements they make to select nominated titles, from small meetings involving library staff only, to larger gatherings. For instance, Hertfordshire Library Service regularly holds a selection meeting attended by around two hundred people. Those at the meeting include not only librarians but also teachers, parents, English advisers and, in recent years, children. The presence of these young people has not yet made a significant impression on the final voting for the three books to go to the selection committee: it is worth noting, though, that one of the books on the Hertfordshire list in 1984 was Bernard Ashley's *Your Guess is as Good as Mine*, a book intended for a younger age range than that which generally receives the Carnegie Medal. This book received only thirteen votes in the final voting, not enough to take it into the top three, but of these thirteen votes, nine were from children.

This brings us back to the idea posed in the title of the

chapter: the books which are given the Carnegie Medal, like those in practically every British children's book award, are chosen by adults for children. This has repercussions throughout the whole of the children's book world, which is dominated by adults, although one counter-argument to this is that it applies to all of the children's manufacturing industries, such as clothing. Children can be involved in the selection of the Carnegie Medal, as in Hertfordshire, but only in a minor way, although since 1969 members of the selection committee do have contact with children. A book's popularity with children is nowhere stated in the guidelines to the Carnegie Medal, as has often been said, although pressure groups have frequently called for its inclusion, as an extraordinary meeting of the YLG decided in 1974. Should the Carnegie Medal have its criteria changed as the Other Award did on its tenth birthday in 1984, when the first of its criteria was that a winning book 'will be accessible, in form and content, to children and young people and will give pleasure and enjoyment'?

The only British children's book award formally to involve children in selection is that introduced by the Federation of Children's Book Groups in 1981. Yet even here there is evidence to show that, in its initial stages, the award is controlled by adults. In America there are twenty-four 'reader's-choice awards' and research has demonstrated that only twenty per cent of the children's books honoured by this type of award has also received an award administered by adults.

But even when a children's book is chosen with children in mind, there are criticisms from some adults. Robert Westall's *The Machine Gunners* was the 1975 Carnegie Medal winner. The selection committee felt it was 'a book definitely written for children and not for a more mature readership' and yet eight children's librarians from the London Borough of Bromley wrote to *Library Association Record* complaining about the book's bad language and violence, asking 'isn't it time that the medal was again awarded to a real children's book as it was originally intended?'

2
'The Great Unread': The Carnegie Books

It would be possible for a researcher to put together a picture of the average winning author of the Carnegie Medal. This has been done in America with the Newbery Medal: one diligent research worker has discovered that the average winner of that award is likely to be a white female, approximately forty-seven years of age and with a college education. Her previous output would be about six novels and 'winning the Newbery Medal is her first literary achievement'. Fascinating though such an exercise is as an intellectual stimulant, it does not tell us very much about the winning books or lead us to guess why they were chosen. For it is possible to see a pattern in the books which have either won or been honoured by the Carnegie Medal, from the searching for quality in the early years of the award to the stabilisation (some would say stagnation) of that quality in the middle years which led to one publishing house monopolising the award. In recent years there has been a great deal of criticism that the winning books have little appeal to children ('the great unread' as one librarian dubbed them) and there have been some attempts to rectify this in the books chosen.

One of the reasons for the introduction of the Carnegie Medal (probably the main reason) was to promote the idea of quality in children's books, to 'mark out really fine work in this field'. This need to raise the level of children's literature was a particular feature of the 1930s when, with a few exceptions, the 'golden age' of the Edwardian period had degenerated into what Robert Leeson has defined as 'the age of brass'. A Library Association Review of 1932 described the scene as 'a few admirable books, submerged in an ocean of terrible trash'. One of the aims of the Carnegie Medal was to revert this trend: 'Quite frankly, many of the books that are written for children are very poor; the field, however, is immense and so, too, should be its opportunities for good authors to distinguish themselves'. This also coincided with other attempts to improve the level of writing for children: both Dent and Oxford University Press appointed children's book editors and *The Junior Bookshelf*, the first British magazine devoted exclusively to the reviewing of children's books, was begun by H. J. B. Woodfield, the library book supplier.

One of the features particularly emphasised in the early years of the Carnegie Medal, which does not seem quite as important today, was that of format. As one of the citations during that period declared: 'The format of *The Radium Woman* is satisfactory. The print is clear, the margins wide and the binding serviceable.' This was particularly important during 'the age of brass' as publishers had become accustomed to producing 'gift books' in editions which invariably promised much more than they were able to give.

However, the main emphasis in the first twenty years of the Carnegie Medal was in honouring writers who had been producing work of a high standard in the years before the introduction of the award. The first winner was, after all, Arthur Ransome, and Kitty Barne and Noel Streatfeild, among others, had produced work of a distinguished standard before they received their medals. The *Library Association Record* editorial which had announced the introduction of the Carnegie Medal had singled out several authors whose works should be emulated. Among these names was that of Walter de la Mare, and in the year this writer was honoured the selection committee did acknowledge that it was giving him a medal for his 'outstanding work in the past for children, both in prose and poetry'. Indeed, de la Mare's *Collected Stories for Children* contained no new material and *The Junior Bookshelf* wryly commented that the precedent which this award set would mean that a reprint of A. A. Milne's *When We Were Very Young* would almost invariably make Milne a Carnegie Medal winner. This system also meant that the 1955 medal went to Eleanor Farjeon, for the selection committee considered it as perhaps the last opportunity it would have 'to recognise appropriately the work of one of the major writers for children of this century'.

The following year was used as an opportunity to honour a writer who had contributed much to children's literature by his books set in Narnia, C. S. Lewis. However, the book which received the award was the final part of his fantasy cycle, *The Last Battle*, and it is the one which is generally regarded as the weakest of the whole series. This does indeed help to enforce criticism of a trait which the selection committee of the award has often been tempted to indulge in, namely recognising a writer's past successes by highlighting a work not up to that writer's usual standard. It happened with Lewis and also with Ransome, the first medal winner, who himself considered *Pigeon Post* to be poor. Although there have been some writers who have won the Carnegie Medal for their first published children's book (for instance, Jan Mark, Robert Westall, Richard Adams), the general trend is to honour an author who has already had several books published. This has meant that some writers have seen a book recognised which posterity has not felt to be their best, and which has missed the freshness and excitement of their early work. On the other hand, it has to be said that there is also a danger in the situation of rewarding a writer whose promise is more fully developed in later work. One of the reasons for the setting up of the *Guardian* Award was to acknowledge new writers and in this it has often been successful as, for instance, with Michelle Magorian's *Goodnight Mister Tom* which was merely commended for the Carnegie Medal. However, the *Guardian* Award's first winner was Leon Garfield, whose book *Devil in the Fog* was honoured. The following year *Smith* was published, and Garfield has continued to produce work of a consistently higher standard than the book which *The Guardian* chose to recognise. Other *Guardian* Award winners, such as Winifred Cawley and Andrew Davies, have failed to live up to their early promise. This whole situation is a type of 'Russian roulette' problem of which all presenters of awards should be aware.

It is perhaps surprising, in view of the different emphases placed on the winners of the *Guardian* Award and the Carnegie Medal respectively, that there has been a good deal of overlap in the winners of both. This is particularly ironic in view of the fact that when Bill Webb (the *Guardian's* literary editor) and John Rowe Townsend introduced their award in 1966, critics of the Carnegie Medal saw the new award as an alternative to the stagnation of the Library Association's recent medal winners. However, in the twenty years of the *Guardian* Award's existence, three books have won both that award and the Carnegie Medal (*Watership Down*, *The Owl Service* and *The Edge of the Cloud*), while six *Guardian* Award winners have been runners up for the Carnegie Medal (Joan Aiken's *The Whispering Mountain*, Gillian Avery's *A Likely Lad*, Peter Dickinson's *The Blue Hawk*, Diana Wynne Jones's *Charmed Life*, Ann Schlee's *The Vandal* and Michelle Magorian's *Goodnight Mister Tom*). This surprised John Rowe Townsend who felt 'there has been more overlap between "The *Guardian*" and "The Carnegie" than I expected' particularly in view of the fact that his award had been introduced because he and Bill Webb believed that an award made and administered by a particular body of people would tend to go to the same kind of book. 'In the three years before we decided to start our award,' writes John Rowe Townsend, 'the Carnegie, as it happened, had been awarded to three successive sound, elegantly written, beautifully produced, Oxford novels, and we wondered, perhaps, if a different perspective might conceivably produce a different kind of winner.'

This concentration on one particular publishing house is typical of the middle period of the Carnegie Medal when, having rewarded authors who had been outstanding before the award was introduced, the selection committee then set out to honour a publisher who produced work of a consistently high standard, Oxford University Press. In 1964, Frank Gardner declared it would be 'a curious year in which neither the Carnegie Medal nor the Kate Greenaway medal went to an

'The Great Unread': The Carnegie Books

O.U.P. book.' In 1958, the Carnegie Medal winner *Tom's Midnight Garden*, and one of the two commended books, Rosemary Sutcliff's *Warrior Scarlet*, were published by Oxford University Press. The firm produced a little paean of praise to itself in its house magazine:

> 'Why did we wander, Kate Greenaway, Greenaway,
> Over the meadow and down in the lane?
> See what they've done while we've been away, been away,
> Oxford have taken our medals again!'
> 'Mr. Carnegie,' said sober Miss Greenaway,
> 'Learn to face facts:' (And he nodded assent)
> 'Oxford have done it before and got clean away;
> No use resisting a yearly event.'

This reliance on one particular publishing house (albeit the one which produced a recognised major classic of children's literature, Philippa Pearce's *Tom's Midnight Garden*) enraged many children's librarians. It also promoted the scorn of critics like Aidan Chambers who in his book *The Reluctant Reader* attacked an Oxford novel, Philip Turner's *The Grange at High Force*, which won the Carnegie Medal in 1965, two years before there were such drastic changes made to the selection procedure of the award.

Chambers felt that *The Grange at High Force* typified 'O.U.P. productions which have figured often of late in the list'. He felt it was 'one of "the well-produced books of good quality" that gives a glow of satisfaction when, dressed in their sparkling plastic covers, they line the library shelves, and the publishers' offices. There in the main they stay.' Chambers also felt that the selection committee had missed a valuable opportunity to honour an outstanding writer by giving the award to Philip Turner's book rather than to Alan Garner for *Elidor* which was a commended book. There is a record of the assessment of *Elidor* and the other winning books by the selection committee for that year. The other books were the medal winner, *The Grange at High Force*, J. G. Fyson's *Journey of the Eldest Son* and Barbara Leonie Picard's *One is One* (which, in fact, was the book most frequently suggested by the library profession as a whole). The elements considered by the selection committee were (i) plot, (ii) characterisation, (iii) style and (iv) format. The committee considered each of the books as follows:

	(i)	(ii)	(iii)	(iv)
Elidor	9	5	8	5
Journey of the Eldest Son	7	5	8	5
One is One	5	8	8	5
The Grange at High Force	10	8	9	3

It can be seen from this table that although *Elidor* is considered superior to *The Grange at High Force* with regard to format (an interesting observation which suggests that the selection committee was not as totally committed to the Oxford University Press house style as has been suggested) and slightly inferior as far as plot and style, its characterisation was felt to be markedly inferior to both the medal winner and *One is One*.

The system of producing a list of commended books was introduced in 1955 and it is helpful in that books can be honoured which, although not outstanding literature, are a significant contribution to children's books. It was, and still is to some extent, a method of highlighting new authors. Thus, in the middle period of the Carnegie Medal, Rosemary Sutcliff, William Mayne, Philippa Pearce and K. M. Peyton were recognised before they became medal winners. One particularly interesting recipient of a highly commended award was the special commendation given to Kathleen Lines's *Lavender's Blue*, illustrated by Harold Jones, in the first year a commended list was introduced. The selection committee had been pressing for some time for the Library Association to introduce a separate award which would honour the illustration of children's books. With the customary delays, the Library Association did not introduce the Kate Greenaway Medal until 1956. The selection committee felt that, in view of these delays, it should draw attention to the qualities of *Lavender's Blue*. While not wishing to denigrate the contribution of Kathleen Lines to this collection of nursery rhymes, it was really Harold Jones whom the selection committee wished to honour. If events had moved more quickly, he would have been the first recipient of the Kate Greenaway Medal rather than Edward Ardizzone who received the award two years later.

Of course it is very easy to make criticisms of previous medal winners with the hindsight of contemporary knowledge and of seeing how children have reacted (or not) to winners. One member of the selection committee which chose *The Grange at High Force* has told me that she can now see the book was a poor choice, but at the time it seemed justifiable. This brings in an important element: how much selection committees for a children's book award have to consider what posterity will make of their judgement.

When the Other Award was introduced by Rosemary Stones and Andrew Mann in 1975, one of the features which the selection panel emphasised was that the award was regarded as an historical one in that it was commending books which were felt to be 'marking a step forward in their time'. This can be seen in the early choices made by the Other Award selection panel, regarded today as dated, particularly in their attitudes to racial politics. Similarly, the first Carnegie Medal winner of the war years, Kitty Barne's *Visitors from London*, was obviously important at the time but is today regarded as patronising in its attitudes to evacuees and nowhere near the author's best work. Not surprisingly, it was the first of the Carnegie Medal winners to go out of print.

Only one book has shared both the Other Award and the Carnegie Medal: Gene Kemp's *The Turbulent Term of Tyke Tiler* (although in very recent years, two Other Award winners, James Watson's *Talking in Whispers* and Robert Swindells' *Brother in the Land* have been highly commended for the Carnegie Medal). The decision to choose Gene Kemp's book is typical of an element which has appeared in the selection of Carnegie Medal books in recent years, although the choice was not popular either with the YLG national committee or with critics like Brian Alderson and Walter McVitty who described *The Turbulent Term of Tyke Tiler* as a 'non-sexist piece of mediocrity'. However, the various selection committees of the 1970s and 1980s have been increasingly forced to consider that medal winners were not popular with children or relevant to their lives.

In 1971, for instance, W. J. Murison, county librarian of West Riding, declared the Carnegie Medal winner, *The God Beneath the Sea*, was an outstanding book but not one for children. Two years later, he attacked *Watership Down* on similar grounds: 'What has now become quite obvious is that the chosen book need appeal only to more intelligent children and adults.' A recent winner, Peter Dickinson's *City of Gold*, was criticised in the columns of *Library Association Record* by a number of librarians who had used the book with children. One correspondent wrote: 'As regards the award in general, why does the committee so often choose something that no "ordinary" child will read? Every year there are books really offering something new and fertile which give children opportunities for growing: every year they are passed by.' (However, this correspondent gives no suggestions of actual books which match these criteria.)

How are the various selection committees able to answer such criticism? Vivien Griffiths, responding to criticisms of *City of Gold*, reiterated that nowhere in the guidelines was it stated that popularity with children should be used as a criterion. Ken Wood, replying to W. J. Murison's criticism, suggested that the terms of reference about what constitutes a child should be reconsidered, rather than the award itself. One YLG chairman, adopting a somewhat patrician tone, declared: 'We are in any case hearing far too often the suggestion that YLG should be looking for easy mediocre reading. This simply is not what the Carnegie is about.' Notwithstanding the way this feeling is expressed, it does have an element of truth in it. The original terms of the Carnegie Medal, and the way these have been expressed in the award's history, do place an emphasis on the literary quality of a winning book. It would be foolish to suggest that a book of this type is going to appeal to a majority of children, any more than anyone would suggest that a winner of the Booker McConnell prize will be read by a large proportion of the adult reading population. There are some Carnegie Medal winners which are popular with children (*The*

'The Great Unread': The Carnegie Books

Borrowers, *The Machine Gunners* and *Tom's Midnight Garden* are examples which spring immediately to mind) but a proportion of the winners is bound to appeal to a minority of readers. But that is no reason to suggest that these books should not have been written, published, or even recognised by an award.

There is evidence to suggest, indeed, that the assumptions made about award-winning books being unpopular with children are spurious. An American librarian who produced a programme to promote Newbery Medal winners in a children's library found that, although there were some books which the children did not like, a significant proportion of the books was read and enjoyed. She also felt that peer acceptance of a book promoted more interest, as did any audiovisual experience (some of the books had been filmed). She concluded that 'few of the Newbery books would ever be read without strong direction and enthusiasm from a teacher or librarian.' In this country, Janet Gaskell carried out a survey of the popularity of award-winning books with 319 children aged between nine and thirteen in North Lancashire schools. She discovered that 82% of the eleven novels which were unknown to the greatest number of children had won an award. However, she concluded there was no evidence to suggest 'that when these novels are read children dislike them. Before I began the study I was convinced that adults choose novels for awards and recommendations which children do not necessarily like, due to the fact that adults use literary criteria, which the children are less concerned with. Ten of the twelve novels in this list of unknown books had won literary awards, and though the vast majority of children are not being told about them, probably because parents and teachers have not been informed either, the few children who tried them did largely enjoy them.'

The members of the Carnegie Medal selection committee are, in fact, in a very difficult situation: on the one hand, they are criticised by librarians and educationalists for not selecting books which are popular with children, and on the other hand the books they honour are condemned by critics of children's literature. Lance Salway exemplified the attitude of the latter when he described most Carnegie Medal winners as 'conventional, solemn, worthy and safe.' It is true to say that, particularly in recent years, innovative, exciting writing for children has been consigned to the highly commended or even commended bracket, but it could be that the various selection committees have felt that this type of writing does not carry the sort of maturity which is consistent with work of a high literary quality. It should also be remembered that the Carnegie Medal is not the only award which has honoured 'worthy' literature.

This situation is indeed one not confined to children's book awards. When William Golding was awarded the 1983 Nobel Prize for Literature, there was some speculation as to why the award had not been given to Graham Greene. The 1982 winner, Gabriel Garcia Marquez, believed the reason for this was that the Swedish Academy could not forgive Greene's use of the language 'for pleasure and entertainment', while the official view was that the Swedish Academy had always shown a preference for writing that was 'more epic and less commercial than Greene's.'

Having charted the various attitudes towards winning books throughout the medal's history and paused to examine the perennial but still important problem of popular versus quality children's literature, it would probably now be interesting to look at the various types of books which have been alternatively honoured or neglected by the Carnegie Medal selection committee.

Non-fiction has never figured prominently in the winners of the medal: only four non-fiction books have ever won the award (the most recent of these being I. W. Cornwall's *The Making of Man* in 1960) while it has rarely been even commended. There have been various disputes about the neglect of information books by the medal selection committees, the most famous being in 1974 when an extraordinary meeting of the YLG committee was called to consider a suggestion from the East Midlands branch of the YLG and from Hertfordshire county library staff that a separate medal should be introduced for non-fiction. This suggestion divided the committee. As a result, the matter was sent back to the branches, with five branches (East Midlands, Northern, South-West, West Midlands, Yorkshire) voting for an additional medal, four (Eastern, North West, Scotland, Wales) against and one abstention (London and Home Counties). This result was reported to the publications committee which rejected the suggestion of two medals on the grounds that it would devalue the existing award. The matter had, in any case, been settled to some extent by the introduction of *The Times Educational Supplement* Information Book Award, first made in 1972 at the instigation of Aidan Chambers. It is probably easy to guess why selection committees have failed to confer the Carnegie Medal on non-fiction books, for the presentation of knowledge tends to date more quickly than imaginative literature does. It is unlikely that a modern child would easily respond to those information books which have won the award.

The introduction of other awards has helped to alleviate the neglect shown to other types of writing. For example, the *Signal* Poetry Award has compensated for the almost total absence of poetry from the major awards, despite the fact that the last twenty years have seen a flowering of talent in this area from such diverse writers as Ted Hughes, Charles Causley and Roger McGough. Plays for children have also been unjustly neglected and there is not yet an award to compensate for this.

Of the imaginative literature which has been the main feature of the Carnegie Medal list, historical fiction is the third most honoured *genre*, although in recent years it has lost its popularity with teachers and librarians and subsequently has not appeared to such a large extent. The two most popular groups are fantasy (which obviously conveys a timeless quality, making it less likely to become dated) and a *genre* which is difficult to classify but which revolves around the lives of young protagonists and their families. In recent years, there have been criticisms that medal winners and honoured books which are intended for an older age range have been selected. At the beginning of the Carnegie Medal's history, W. C. Berwick Sayers had announced that the winning book would be one written for a child somewhere between the ages of nine and twelve and that 'in literary form it should be in the best English; its story should follow the line of the possible, if not the probable; its characters should be alive, its situations credible, and its tone in keeping with the generally accepted standards of good behaviour and right thinking.' However, in 1973, Joan Butler, writing on behalf of Hertfordshire county library staff, wrote to the YLG committee asking for a definition of an age range to be included in the criteria of the award and suggesting that it should be for twelve years of age and under. This may be the reason why the proposed children's book award, the School Library Association's Peter Pan Award, and the Smarties Prize (inaugurated in 1985), have concentrated on the younger age range. A previous Carnegie Medal panel member has observed that it is impossible to try to equate a short, well-written book for the seven to eight age group with a long, well developed and high quality novel for teenagers. I observed this myself at the 1984 selection meetings where one of the contenders for the award was Dick King-Smith's *The Sheep Pig* which had already won the *Guardian* Award. Some of the panel members appeared to believe that as the book was of necessity more simple in its development than others on the list, it was therefore of lesser quality. However, it is not just the Carnegie Medal which is guilty of this assumption: when Jane Gardam's *The Hollow Land* won the Whitbread Award in 1981, Nancy Chambers observed that she would much rather the award had gone to the same author's *Bridget and William* for 'it takes more than just talent to write specifically for 7–8 year olds and produce in a few thousand words, a beautifully shaped story that is both literary and entirely accessible to an inexperienced audience.'

Probably the question most asked about the Carnegie Medal is: 'How many masterpieces of children's literature have failed to get the award?' Of course, one person's idea of a masterpiece is not necessarily another's but there are several notable books which the selection committees have ignored. Possibly the most quoted is Tolkien's *The Hobbit* which appeared in the second year of the medal's history, when the award went to Eve Garnett's *The Family from One End Street*, in its time an innovative book. Records from this era are so thin that it is impossible to judge whether *The Hobbit* was considered by the selection committee or ignored, although the latter seems unlikely in view of the fact that the book had been favourably received by reviewers. However, Tolkien was awarded the *New York Herald Tribune* Prize for the best juvenile book of the season. With this prize came a cheque for $250 which was probably more welcome to the writer at this stage in his career than an award which had yet to prove its worth and which carried no monetary value.

One book which had appeared on the initial list of books suggested by the library profession for consideration in 1968 was Ted Hughes's *The Iron Man*. This most popular book for the junior age range was discarded in favour of Rosemary Harris's *The Moon in the Cloud* (which readership surveys show to be an extremely unpopular book with children) and a commended list of Joan Aiken, Margaret Balderson and Leon Garfield. Even more curiously, it was ignored at a time in the medal's history when there was some consternation among the library profession that books for younger children were not getting enough attention in the awards. Had *The Iron Man* won the Carnegie Medal it is a choice which would have doubtless also satisfied the critics: John Rowe Townsend, for example, has called it 'one of the most remarkable of younger children's books to appear in recent years'.

Four more modern books which were neglected by the Carnegie Medal selection committee, despite the fact that several of them appeared on the initial list of suggestions from the library profession, were the books which comprised Alan Garner's *Stone Book* quartet. It may be possible, however, to suggest why these books, which Humphrey Carpenter has stated are worthy to be considered beside the Victorian and Edwardian masterpieces of children's literature, were ignored by the various selection committees. For one thing, they appeared over several years and so it would be difficult invidiously to divide up the work and give the award to only one of the books. This is one situation where an award given for the opus of an author's work rather than for just one book, such as the suggested Colwell Medal, would be of use. It could also be said that the *Stone Book* quartet appeared at the wrong stage of the Carnegie Medal's history for the books to be recognised. They were published at a time when the selection committees were making efforts to honour books which were immediately accessible to children. For instance, in the year *Tom Fobble's Day*, which many critics believe to be the most masterly in the quartet, was published, the Carnegie Medal winner was *The Turbulent Term of Tyke Tiler*. Many librarians and teachers believe that Alan Garner's books are not enjoyed by children, despite the fact that there are numerous cases of children from many different ages and backgrounds responding positively to the *Stone Book* quartet. The books themselves are difficult to classify: they are short, written often in dialect and are not obviously for one particular age range. They would probably need the intervention of a teacher or librarian to promote them but, as we have said before, so would many other award-winning books.

In discovering the qualities of individual books, it is extremely difficult to obliterate personal preferences. I have found it almost impossible to write this chapter without showing my own prejudices, for there are some Carnegie Medal winners which I feel are of little quality while there are some which in my opinion are exactly the right choice. As John Rowe Townsend has said, when discussing the winners of the Newbery Medal: 'No sensible commentator would expect to find a list that fitted his own prescription exactly; everyone would agree that, with benefit of hindsight, it would be pleasant (though clearly impracticable) to reshape the list, remove the weaker titles, and bring in books that now seem to have been mistakenly passed over. No two people would agree on what books should be discarded or introduced.'

Discussion of winning books may be idiosyncratic but there has been discussion of how the Carnegie Medal winners have been publicised and promoted which suggests that, in this case, there are vast areas for improvement.

3
Getting the Carnegie Medal Publicised

From the beginning of its history the Carnegie Medal has had problems about publicity, although in its early years the impression was given that the Library Association went out of its way to avoid attracting attention. For many years, the medal itself was presented within the confines of the Association's Council. 'It would have been better to send the blessed thing by post,' complained the first medal winner, Arthur Ransome, after he had been presented with his medal by a former schoolfellow, the Archbishop of York, the Library Association President for that year. One would have thought that the Association itself would feel committed to give publicity to its own award but in the first two years after the Carnegie Medal was first given, the *Library Association Record* did not even announce the winners. This lack of publicity continued well into the war years, with Eleanor Graham complaining in 1944 that mention of the medal struck no note of enthusiasm from the 'average bookseller'; while during the same year Eileen Colwell wrote: 'And when the award has been decided, how do librarians, booksellers and publishers advertise it? Scarcely at all. Surely if the award is worth anything, if it is to be a fitting memorial to the benefactor whose name it bears, it should arouse widespread public interest. It needs to be written and talked about, advertised in all libraries and bookshops and awarded with some ceremony.'

Events moved slowly to improve this situation but it would appear that this was often against the wishes of the Library Association hierarchy. In 1954 the medal was presented at a press conference but this was not with the approval of the Association's conference sub-committee. Two years earlier, the Youth Libraries Section had suggested that Phyllis Parrott should introduce the winning author, but the conference sub-committee had decided its representative, Edgar Osborne, would be the best person to do this. At the 1954 press conference Phyllis Parrott did finally get to introduce the winning author (Edward Osmond), and the whole event was considered to be successful enough to be repeated the following year but was dropped in 1956 by orders of the Library Association Council.

It was decided that 1957 should be celebrated to mark the twenty-first anniversary of the first presentation of the Carnegie Medal. The committee felt that this anniversary should be honoured by two special events: a commemorative book and a celebratory meal. In May, 1956, Eileen Colwell had suggested the idea of 'a commemorative booklet' and the following month Marcus Crouch was invited to undertake the editorship of what was to become *Chosen for Children*. Crouch deliberately modelled the book on the American work, *Newbery Medal Books: 1922–1955*, and he used the pattern of an introductory passage about each book, followed by an extract from the particular book and a comment from each author. Of the nineteen winning authors, three, Eleanor Doorly, Kitty Barne and Walter de la Mare, were dead, Arthur Ransome was too old to make a comment and C. S. Lewis showed no interest in the project. The text was ready by the end of February, 1957, and two thousand copies were printed. However, at the final stages of the book, Crouch found himself in disagreement with the Library Association on a number of points and asked for his name to be removed. In fact, his name does not appear on the title page of either the first or second editions, but the acknowledgements thank him for 'compiling' the book.

Although Crouch was not able to receive the credit for *Chosen for Children*, his feelings about the Carnegie Medal are still very much in evidence, not least in the book's introduction. It is here that he tackles the view that the winning books appeal to a limited audience. Crouch responds 'this is to apply the democratic principle blindly.' The medal is not awarded as the result of a plebiscite, he avers it is made by 'a small body of experts' to a work which 'receives the commendation of discriminating readers'. This was a commonly shared feeling at the time, inspired as it was by the views of two children's writers. Walter de la Mare believed that only the best was good enough for children, while C. S. Lewis claimed that a good children's book was one that was worth reading at the age of fifty. Although this may seem incongruous in our child-centred society today, it is noteworthy that this view, particularly when applied to children's book awards, is one which has not been replaced by a more democratic view.

Crouch also claimed at the very conclusion of his views on the Carnegie Medal that one of the wishes of the medal's originators had been satisfied: 'There have been marked improvements since 1936 in the general standard of publishing and reviewing children's books. It is not too much to claim that this is attributable in part to an acceptance of the high standards established by the Carnegie Medal.'

It was decided to hold the celebratory lunch at the Dorchester Hotel on the 27th November, 1957. The committee felt that 'in view of the importance of the occasion', the Queen Mother or Princess Margaret might accept an invitation to attend. Obviously the Royal Family did not regard the occasion with such importance as they were unable to accept this invitation. However, 128 people attended the luncheon, including twelve medal winners. The speakers were Sir Edward Boyle, Parliamentary Secretary to the Ministry of Education, Dr. Jacob Bronowski, President of the Library Association for that year, Ian Parsons, President of the Publishers Association, Edward Ardizzone and Noel Streatfeild. The latter said she felt the medal was a great thing to win but complained that she did not know what to do with it as it was 'too light for a paper-weight, and certainly not decorative.'

The celebratory luncheon was obviously considered a great success but it was to be seven years before a similar event was arranged. In 1964 the Children's Book Circle (an informal association of publishers) invited the Library Association to announce the medal winners at the Circle's annual dinner. The whole ceremony was shrouded in secrecy and the names of the medal winners were not even written down in the committee minutes. Some measure of success was achieved: the BBC televised an edited version and *The Bookseller* devoted six pages to the event. The secrecy introduced at this event became a regular feature of the awarding of the Carnegie Medal and was only dropped after the sweeping changes of 1968: the reason for this was that the secrecy had become something of a farcical situation with, for instance, many people arriving at the 1968 presentation knowing that the winner was going to be *The Owl Service*. However, the element of secrecy was reintroduced in 1985 with some success, perhaps because it had become a regular feature of book award ceremonies such as the Booker McConnell and the Whitbread awards.

During the late 1960s and early 1970s a few attempts were made to generate publicity about the Carnegie Medal. The Youth Libraries Group committee suggested that book tokens be presented for commended books (£5.5s. for highly commended, £3.3s. for commended) but this suggestion, reminiscent of schoolday prize giving, was amended to the presentation of certificates. In 1969 the committee introduced bookmarkers which carried a list of former medal winners and gold stickers in the shape of an imitation medal which could be fixed by publishers to the jacket of a winning book.

In April, 1970, the complete short list was announced, the first time this had been done. However, when the final list was completed, those authors and illustrators who had been on the short list but were not on the final list expressed their disappointment with some vehemence. Publishers complained, and Brian Alderson, writing in *The Times*, defined it as dividing 'not only sheep from goats, but also sheep from sheep'. The idea of a public short list was dropped until the 1980s when it had gained respectability as a method of announcing award winning books. The presentation was also altered in 1970. Instead of the usual 'fork supper' announcement which had been the norm after the successful 1964 Children's Book Circle meeting, it was decided that the presentation would be made on the Friday

Getting the Carnegie Medal Publicised

evening prior to the Library Association's annual conference.

One innovation which was introduced in 1970 was the printing of posters publicising the winner. These were printed by The Bodley Head. Various alternatives were tried for the presentation ceremony, such as at a dinner in London in 1971, at a luncheon in Birmingham in 1973 and finally at one night of the YLG weekend school which was first tried in 1974 and is now the current norm. However, the publicity which these events generated was small enough to warrant a letter from Leon Garfield, chairman of the children's writers group of the Society of Authors, suggesting the use of the public relations committee of the Children's Book Group. YLG wrote to the publications committee, strongly supporting this suggestion. The success of this liaison can be judged by the appearance of news items the following year in both the *Daily Mirror* and *The Sunday Times*. The lack of general publicity was not aided by the *Library Association Record's* refusal to publish articles on the medal winners in both 1971 and 1972 because the editor felt that the Youth Libraries Group should pay for its own space.

However, despite these and any subsequent efforts to generate public interest in the award, it could be said with justification that the Carnegie Medal is little known even to those who have an interest in children's literature. Are there any examples of a children's book award which promotes wide publicity or should the Youth Libraries Group resign itself to the fact that this lack of knowledge is likely to be the permanent situation as far as the medal is concerned?

Probably the most consistently publicised children's book award in Great Britain is the Whitbread Award. The children's book category is one of five in the award: each category winner now receives a prize of £1000 (previously £3000) and is eligible for the overall Whitbread Book-of-the-Year prize of £17,500. In 1978, six years after the Whitbread Award began, Samuel Whitbread, Chairman of the firm, pronounced that their award was 'probably now the leading award in children's books' but it is difficult to justify this view from the list of winners. This is a motley collection of titles ranging from picture books like *The Butterfly Ball* and Russell Hoban's *How Tom Beat Captain Najork and His Hired Sportsmen*, through books which are not necessarily their author's best work (Penelope Lively's *A Stitch in Time*, Jill Paton Walsh's *The Emperor's Winding Sheet*), to books which are very curious winners indeed (W. J. Corbett's *The Song of Pentecost*, Shelagh Macdonald's *No End to Yesterday*). Only once has the Carnegie Medal winner and the Whitbread Award winner coincided: in 1979 with Peter Dickinson's *Tulku*, although two Whitbread winners, Jane Gardam's *The Hollow Land* and Philippa Pearce's *The Battle of Bubble and Squeak*, were both commended by the Carnegie selection committee.

The awards dinner is an event which, in the case of the Booker and Whitbread, has sometimes been televised. The Carnegie Medal also is presented at a dinner during the Youth Libraries Group weekend school, and announced at a daytime ceremony a few months before the dinner. These are very pleasant and enjoyable events, but there is as yet not enough drama involved to have them televised. The banquet at which the Newbery and Caldecott Medals are presented in America is a far more sumptuous affair. For instance, the 1984 ceremony was attended by around 1,200 people. A dinner at beautifully decorated tables in a large hotel, and a souvenir programme and tape recording of the acceptance speeches for each guest, were provided at a cost of about £25 per head. It would be possible for the Youth Libraries Group to organise a similar event, but the likelihood that over a thousand people would pay this price for a ticket is exceptionally remote.

The Newbery Medal's publicity is always mentioned as a shining example to the promoters of the Carnegie Medal. This is probably because of the effects the announcement of the American award has on sales of the winning book. In the year immediately following its being awarded the Newbery Medal, the winning book is expected to sell 50,000 copies, with honour books selling between 10,000 and 20,000 copies as well, a pattern which is repeated in countries like Japan and Australia. However, it could be said that this situation means that librarians in these countries are more willing to follow the dictates of others, rather than make up their own minds. It is important, also, to put the sales figures in context for, as one

American award-winning publisher has calculated, the sales of these books amount to less than one per cent of the total children's book sales in a year. Penelope Lively, winner of the Carnegie Medal and the Whitbread Award, found that sales were good for *The Ghost of Thomas Kempe*, the Carnegie Medal winner. However, she felt that they would have been good anyway for this particular book, whereas *A Stitch in Time*, the Whitbread Award winner, and a very different type of book, had not sold particularly well. She did feel, however, that the Carnegie Medal did 'a great deal to help a book on its way.'

The effect of a children's book award on sales is an important element in the publicity that award generates. This is perhaps regrettable to some book lovers but it is a fact of life, one that is even more important in the world of adult book awards. The Booker McConnell prize does help to sell copies of the short-listed books: the cumulative sales of the 1984 winner, Anita Brookner's *Hotel du Lac*, leapt by over thirteen thousand during the week in which the prize was announced. However, this situation is not at all similar in the world of children's books, for unlike adult hardback fiction which has a market (albeit a small one) with personal buyers, children's hardback fiction is almost totally purchased by libraries and schools. Sales and the size of the prize money are important factors in the amount of publicity an adult book award receives. It is surely not a coincidence that when it was announced that the prize for the Betty Trask Award for romantic fiction would be increased to £12,000, the prize money given for the Booker prize was raised to £15,000. The Booker is the most publicised of all British literary awards, having been televised for a number of years. It ought to be pointed out, however, that the ceremony is televised on the minority channels (BBC 2 or Channel 4) thus perpetuating the myth that reading is a minority interest.

It will be interesting to see if the Smarties Prize does the same for the children's book world as the Booker does for the adult, as many of its supporters have claimed it will do. Certainly its launching received some attention in a number of the daily newspapers, including a long item in the *Financial Times*, and in magazines like *Junior Education*, *Mother* and *Nursery World*. Will the Smarties Prize and the new-style Whitbread attract more attention, and will they have a miraculous effect on the sales of winning children's books? And if they do, how will that affect the Carnegie Medal with no cash prize and its somewhat tarnished reputation?

Conclusion

This work has so far looked at the Carnegie Medal from the viewpoint of those involved with children's books, librarians, critics and publishers for instance, but rarely from that of the people who are most directly concerned with the creation of children's literature, namely the authors. What are their feelings about the award? It is salutary to read Lucy M. Boston's account of her medal award in 1962, for *A Stranger at Green Knowe*. She writes, in her autobiography, *Memory in a House*, that at first the Carnegie Medal did not strike her

> . . . as a dizzy peak. However my publishers wrote ardent congratulations, and letters from the awarding body of librarians wrote awesomely of the "supreme award". I was gradually coaxed away by such professional shibboleths from my common sense. I began to feel perhaps I had done something good, and that it was arrogant to depreciate an award. And not only one's vanity but one's proper pride as an artist longs to believe in recognition.

Having been told that she would have to make an acceptance speech to the audience and press, Lucy Boston took pains to write and learn one, only to be informed when she arrived at the ceremony that she would be unable to give her speech. The presentation itself was made at the Library Association's annual conference, held that year in Llandudno:

> The stage of the Pavilion had last been used for a drawing room comedy and the set was still there. Against this background we were placed together at the end of a row of chairs and left there as if in our prams for a very long time. I

watched the auditorium filling up and searched the gallery for photographer's equipment or spotlights, and the floor for a table for the press. There was neither. I wonder who had thought up that particular torment for me.

Finally the functionaries filed in to take their places though without any welcome for us, and we all stood up for the entry of His Worship the Mayor. He talked with outrageous vulgarity for half an hour about the amusements, amenities and funfairs of Llandudno and the excellent hat shops and hairdressers where the ladies would want to enjoy themselves, while hubby was at the conference. I think he can never have read a book and probably didn't know or care what particular conference he was opening. Last week it had been Labour and the following week was perhaps the British Dental Association. I wonder if they all got the same speech. Why not? I thought of my chosen words for which there was no time. With relief we all stood up to see him out.

There followed perhaps an hour of reading the minutes, the schedule and rules of the conference, and paying compliments to retiring members. The Head Librarian of the British Museum was awarded a certificate of good behaviour by proxy – he was wisely not present – and then our two sponsors said their pieces. I was assured that my book was really quite up to the required standard. We [i.e. Lucy Boston and the Kate Greenaway Medal winner] received our medals like school children and said our brief thanks, and all was over for us. While the other business continued we compared our medals with incredulity. Mine was almost exactly like the one I got for swimming the mile when I was eleven. His was not even as adult as that. Of course the medals were only symbols, but of what?

Later I sat beside the President for the official luncheon. It was clear that children's books were so far below his interest that he had neglected to inform himself about this last unnecessary addition to them. Beyond saying he believed I had written a book he risked no conversation at all to my side, having some easier neighbour on his left. It was an excellent meal and I gave it my attention.

Conclusion

In recent years, it is to be hoped that the experience and feelings of prize-winners would be more likely to concur with Jan Mark's reactions to receiving the medal for the second time for *Handles*:

> Youth librarians are possibly better read than any other branch of their profession. However partial their judgement, it is still likely to be an honest one and it is this that makes the Carnegie, professionally speaking, the most valuable award of all. It is in the gift of readers. As one who writes in order to be read, there is no one's commendation I value more.

Notwithstanding the fact that this opinion is of necessity biased (Jan Mark is hardly likely to condemn the medal and its selectors on such an occasion), the sentiment it expresses does contain an element of possibly the most important reason why the Carnegie Medal should remain in existence. Unlike other British awards, the potential winners of the Library Association's children's book awards are any of the children's books published each year which can be recommended by any of the country's librarians. The panel which selects the books consists of a number of people who know of children's books and of children's reactions to books. There seems to be a feeling subtly expressed by critics that librarians are the wrong people to select award-winning books. But why should this be the case? Why are they considered inferior to other panels which for the most part contain children's authors whose motives may be considered not totally altruistic, and who are often ignorant of developments in children's literature? This vast scope in the availability of suggestions for winning books and in the range and knowledge of the selection panel is one for which the Youth Libraries Group and its predecessors fought long and hard, and it is one of the aspects which makes the Carnegie Medal important.

But if the Carnegie Medal *is* important, then how should this importance be proclaimed? It is difficult to justify the abysmal ignorance of a fifty-year-old award from those groups who should be expected to know something about it. Of course there is no one simple solution to stimulating more publicity for the award. For publicity to be effective there has to be some money generated and the finances of the Carnegie Medal have often resulted in little spare cash being available for publicity. The fact that the award carries no financial reward for the winning author is a big disadvantage as far as publicity is concerned. However, there are small things which could be done to generate some excitement. The date when the winning book is announced should be made known to at least the whole library profession, and not just to the *cognoscenti* who attend the announcement ceremony. The ceremony itself could be more open, as indeed is that at which the Other Award winners are announced, and panel members should be prepared to justify their selections to members of the public. The names of the selection panel should always be published, as they were at one time. 'I've never met a librarian who would admit to having been on the Carnegie Medal selection committee,' a children's book editor once said to me, but in fact a large number of eminent children's librarians have sat on the panel, including those who have made a name for themselves in other areas of children's literature, such as Judith Elkin and Sheila Ray.

As for the winning books themselves, it is an interesting exercise to swap around books on past lists, to remove worthy but dull works which have appeared, to replace ephemeral material with books which have stood the test of time: but this is only a party game. It would be a very bland list of titles which earned the approbation of everyone and children's books are as subject to the vagaries of fashion as any other form of the arts. Nor are the various selection committees which have chosen Carnegie Medal winners the only award-winning bodies which have presented prizes to second-rate material: even the illustrious Oscars have gone to films more worthy of oblivion than recognition. It may seem to be damning the Carnegie Medal with faint praise to say that if some of the books honoured are no better than those recognised by other children's book awards then they are certainly no worse: but it would be true. What the Youth Libraries Group must constantly try to highlight in its selections, however, is literary quality, for that is intrinsic to the criteria of the Carnegie Medal. It must also accept that books of this quality may not be widely popular with children. Nevertheless, quality and talent are what keep children's books exciting and these must be supported and encouraged in every possible way.

What of the future of the Carnegie Medal? Will it still be awarded in fifty years time, assuming that technology has not killed off the book? Evidence from France suggests that the French, for many years promoters of book awards, have become blasé about them. For instance, the world-renowned Prix Goncourt was in 1984 given to Marguerite Duras, an established writer, for an autobiography rather than a novel. This was seen by the French establishment as a signal that the award was losing its importance, especially as Mme. Duras had expressed her total indifference to literary awards. Perhaps the same will happen in Great Britain.

I feel I should end on a note of warning. It seems to me to be dangerous to attach too much importance to the presenting of any prize. The administering body of any award, from the Nobel Prize to a local flower show, is treading a dangerous path, for it is saying that one article is superior to another when one may be intrinsically different with a subtly unusual set of qualities. To dispense judgement from on high and class one better than another smacks of the ridiculous. Where children's book awards are vital is in bringing children and books together as often as possible: the goal for which we should all be working. If a child's life has been in some way altered by that child reading *Tom's Midnight Garden*, or even an 'unpopular' book like *The God Beneath the Sea*, then the fifty years of the Carnegie Medal, with all its tribulations, turmoils and arguments, will definitely have been worthwhile.

Bibliography

ABORNE, Carlene. The Newberys: getting them read (it isn't easy). *Library Journal*, 99 (8) 15 April 1974, pp. 1195–7
ALDERSON, Brian. Looking to literary laurels in books for the young. *The Times*, 6 June 1973, p. 10
—Medals for books. *The Times*, 6 May 1970, p. 13
—Puritanism raises its uninspiring head in literature for children. *The Times*, 24 September, 1975, p. 10
—Some quality still outstanding. *The Times*, 26 July 1978, p. 12
ARISTIDES. Scares in the story corner. *Times Educational Supplement*, 2 July 1982, p. 68
BACKHOUSE, Roger. The world is bored with merit. *Library Association Record*, 86 (2), February 1984, p. 67
BARKER, Keith. The books kids like. *School Libraries Group News* 11, pp. 20–1
—The Carnegie Medal: a critical history and examination of the award given annually by librarians for an outstanding book written in English for children. Unpublished dissertation, University of Wales, 1985
—Going for gold. *Library Association Record*, 85 (9), September 1983, p. 310
BAUER, Carolyn J. and SANBORN, LaVonne H. The best of both worlds: children's books acclaimed by adults and young readers. *Top of the News*, 38 (1), Fall 1981, pp. 53–6
BOOKPOST. *Signal* 30, September 1979, pp. 171–6; 31, January 1980, pp. 57–60; 32, May 1980, pp. 114–22; *Signal* 37, January 1982, pp. 52–7
BOSTON, L.M. *Memory in a House*. London: Bodley Head, 1973
BOWEN, Elizabeth. Children's books: the endless debate. *Library Association Record*, 78 (7), July 1976, p. 313
BRADMAN, Tony and TRIGGS, Pat. The awards business. *Books for Keeps*, 20 May 1983, pp. 4–5.

Bibliography

BROGAN, Hugh. *The Life of Arthur Ransome*. London: Cape, 1984

CARPENTER, Humphrey. *J. R. R. Tolkien: a biography*. London: Allen & Unwin, 1977

—*Secret Gardens: a study of the golden age of children's literature*. London: Allen & Unwin, 1985

CHAMBERS, Aidan. *The Reluctant Reader*. Oxford: Pergamon, 1969

Chosen for Children. London: The Library Association, 1957; 2nd edn, 1967

COLWELL, Eileen. The L.A. Carnegie medal. *Library Association Record*, 46 (1), January 1944, pp. 14–15

—The radium woman. *Library Association Record*, 43 (1), January 1941, p. 7

Coming of age. *Junior Bookshelf*, 21 (4), November 1957, pp. 243–9

Criticism and the consumer. *Library Association Record*, 79 (4), April 1977, p. 169

CROUCH, Marcus. Salute to children's literature and its creators: 21st birthday for Carnegie Medal. *Top of the News*, 14 May 1958, pp. 7–10

—ELLIS, Alec, eds. *Chosen for Children*, 3rd edn. London: The Library Association, 1977

DOHM, Janice H. Newbery and Carnegie awards. *Junior Bookshelf*, 21 (1), January 1957, pp. 5–15

Editorial. *Library Association Record*, 39 (1), January 1937, p. 1

ELLIS, Alec. 40 years of the Carnegie Medal: a hallmark of quality. *Library Association Record*, 79 (2), February 1977, pp. 76–7, 92

—*A History of Children's Reading and Literature*, Oxford: Pergamon, 1968

EPSTEIN, Jason. 'Good bunnies always obey': books for American children, in EGOFF, Sheila *et al.* (eds.), *Only Connect: readings on children's literature*, 2nd edn, Toronto: O.U.P., 1980, pp. 79–94

EVANS, Bryan. Selection process for Carnegie and Greenaway awards. *Library Association Record*, 81 (3), March 1979, pp. 120–1

Bibliography

FARJEON, Annabel. *Morning Has Broken: A biography of Eleanor Farjeon* London: Julia MacRae Books, 1986

GARDNER, F. M. The President's page.*Library Association Record*, 66 (6), June 1964, p. 268

GASKELL, Janet. The response of children in the middle years age range to prestige children's literature. Unpublished dissertation, University of Lancaster, 1980

GRAHAM, Eleanor. The Carnegie Medal and its winners. *Junior Bookshelf*, 8 (2), July 1944, pp. 59–65

HEEKS, Peggy. A different background. *The Bookseller*, no. 3308, 17 May 1969, pp. 2482–4

—Looking for a winner. *Times Literary Supplement*, 6 June 1968, p. 578

HIBBERD, Dominic. The Flambards trilogy: objections to a winner. *Children's Literature in Education*, 8, July 1972, pp. 5–15

HILL, Janet. *Children are people: the librarian in the community*. London: Hamish Hamilton, 1973

HOFFMAN, Mary. Honour and glory. *Times Educational Supplement*, 30 September 1983, pp. 44–6

—A judge's story. *Times Educational Supplement*, 2 October, 1981, pp. 20–1

—Winning ways. *Times Educational Supplement*, 23 July 1976, p.47

HUNT, Peter. Criticism and children's literature. *Signal*, 15, September 1974, pp. 117–30

—Whatever happened to Jan Mark? *Signal*, 31, January 1980, pp.11–19

HUTTON, M. A clutch of Carnegies. *The School Librarian*, 11 (5), July 1963, pp. 461–4

JONES, Dolores Blythe. *Children's Literature Awards and Winners: a directory of prizes, authors and illustrators*. Detroit: Neal-Schuman, 1983

JORDAN, Helen L. State awards for children's books. *Top of the News*, 36 (1), Fall 1979, pp. 79–86

Junior Bookshelf. 1 (2), 1937, p. 28; 1 (4), 1937, p. 17; 6 (2), 1942, p. 59; 12 (1), 1948, p. 31

KAYDEN, Mimi and GLAZER, Suzanne M. For whom the calls

toll: the Newbery-Caldecott awards from the publishers' viewpoint. *Top of the News*, 36 (1), Fall 1979, pp. 35–42

KINGMAN, Lee, (ed.), *Newbery and Caldecott Medal Books: 1956–1965*. Boston: The Horn Book, 1965

—*Newbery and Caldecott Medal Books 1966–1975*. Boston: The Horn Book, 1975

KNUDSEN, Grethe. The perennial question – more or fewer awards? *Reading Time*, 85, October, 1982, pp. 14–16

LEESON, Robert. *Reading and Righting*. London: Collins, 1985

A librarian. A poor thin way of doing things. *Junior Bookshelf*, 31 (4), 1967, pp. 229–30

Library Association. Study School and National Conference Proceedings 1978. London: The Library Association, 1978

Library Association Carnegie Medal. *Library Association Record*, 43 (1), January 1941, p. 8

Library Association Record. Correspondence: 68 (8), August 1966, p. 312; 68 (10), October 1966, pp. 377–8; 71 (1), January 1969, p. 26; 73 (8), August 1971, p. 162; 73 (10), October 1971, p. 201; 75 (7), July 1973, p. 144; 75 (8), August 1973, pp. 166–7; 75 (9), September 1973, pp. 182–3; 78 (10), October 1976, p. 497; 79 (4), April 1977, p. 220; 83 (9), September 1981, p. 441; 83 (11), November 1981, p. 540; 84 (3), March 1982, p. 111; 84 (5), May 1982, p. 197

LIVELY, Penelope. [unnamed article]. *Author*, 90 (2), Summer 1979, pp. 70–1

MACON, Myra and BAGGETT, Carolyn. The Newberys: a diversionary approach. *Top of the News*, 36 (4), Summer 1980, pp. 375–9

McVITTY, Walter. Children's book awards. *Reading Time*, 74, January 1980, pp. 4–15

—Children's book awards: what you don't know about them. *Australian School Librarian*, 9 (4), December 1972, pp. 6–14

—The effect of children's book awards. *Reading Time*, 85, October 1982, pp. 16–19

MANN, Andrew. The Other Award. *Signal*, 18, September 1975, pp. 142–5

MANNING, Rosemary. Whatever happened to Onion John? *Times Literary Supplement*, 4 December 1969, pp. 1383–4

Bibliography

MORANSEE, Jess R., (ed.). *Children's Prize Books: an international listing of 193 children's literature prizes.* Munich: Saur, 1983

Noblesse and much obliged. *Guardian*, 8 October 1983, p. 5

Notes from the attic. *Junior Bookshelf*, 1 (3), 1937, p. 21

PETERSON, Linda Kauffman and SOLT, Marilyn Leathers. *Newbery and Caldecott Medal and Honor Books: an annotated bibliography.* Boston: G.K. Hall, 1982

Prize-winning children's books. *The Bookseller*, no. 3048, 23 May 1964, pp. 1962–4.

RAY, Colin. 'The edge of the cloud' – a reply to Dominic Hibberd. *Children's Literature in Education*, 9 November 1972, pp. 5–6

SALWAY, Lance. Kids' Oscars. *Times Literary Supplement*, 16 July 1976, p. 888

SAYERS, W. C. Berwick. The Library Association Carnegie Medal and Mr. Arthur Ransome. *Library Association Record*, 39 (5), May 1937, pp. 218–9

SCHMIDT, Dorothy J. and OSBORN, Jeanne. The effect of literary awards on children's book recommendations. *Top of the News*, 31 (2), April 1974, pp. 257–66

SMITH, Irene. *A History of the Newbery and Caldecott Medals.* New York: Viking Press, 1957

STEVENSON, W. B. What the judges are looking for. *The Bookseller*, no. 3048, 23 May 1964. pp. 1964–6

Times Literary Supplement. Correspondence: 20 June 1968, p. 649; 27 June 1968, p. 679; 11 July 1968, p. 729; 18 July 1968, p. 753

TOWNSEND, John Rowe. A decade of Newbery books in perspective, in KINGMAN, Lee (ed.), *Newbery and Caldecott Medal Books 1966–1975.* Boston: The Horn Book, 1975, pp. 141–53

—Standard of criticism for children's literature, in CHAMBERS, Nancy (ed.), *The Signal Approach to Children's Books.* Harmondsworth: Kestrel 1980, pp. 193–207

—Ten years of the *Guardian* Award, in Federation of Children's Book Groups Year Book 1978–79, pp. 14–15

—*Written for Children: an outline of English-language children's literature.* 2nd rev. edn, Harmondsworth: Kestrel, 1983

Bibliography

TREASE, Geoffrey. The revolution in children's literature, in BLISHEN, Edward (ed.), *The Thorny Paradise: writers on writing for children*. Harmondsworth: Kestrel, 1975. pp. 13–24

WESTALL, Robert. How real do you want your realism? *Signal*, 28, January 1979, pp. 34–46

Whitbread Literary Awards. *The Bookseller*, 9 December 1978, p. 3453

APPENDIX A

Chronological History of the Carnegie Medal

1935 Suggested a medal should be awarded in honour of Andrew Carnegie.

1936 Decided this medal would be given for 'best children's book'.

1937 First medal given to Arthur Ransome.

1940 Eileen Colwell on the selection committee, representing the Association of Children's Librarians. Criteria published and 'best book' replaced by 'an outstanding book'.

1944 Award withheld.

1946 Award withheld.

1949 Youth Libraries Section recommended more involvement of children's librarians.

1952 W. C. Berwick Sayers on the committee for the last time.

1954 Medal presented at a press conference.

1955 List of commended books issued.

1957 Twenty-first anniversary of the first presentation of the medal. There was a celebratory meal and *Chosen for Children* was published.

1964 Medals announced at the Children's Book Circle's annual dinner amid great secrecy.

Appendix A

1966 The *Guardian* Award established. Youth Libraries Group to submit list of six to twelve titles to selection committee of Carnegie Medal. YLG established equal number of representatives on that committee.

1967 Award withheld. Eileen Colwell on committee for last time and Janet Hill for first (and only) time. Second edition of *Chosen for Children* published. Certificates presented to commended authors.

1968 Correspondence in *Times Literary Supplement*. Terms of award clarified so that an author could win more than once.

1969 Selection committee consisted solely of representatives of YLG.

1970 Medal presented at Library Association's annual conference. Short list announced. YLG would not have to obtain approval of winning titles by the publications committee.

1971 Criticism that winners 'not for children'.

1973 YLG branches invited to nominate selection committee members.

1974 Medal presented at YLG weekend school.

1975 The Other Award introduced.

1977 Third edition of *Chosen for Children*. Marcus Crouch (in conjunction with Alec Ellis) recognised as author.

1978 Working party set up to examine promotion and presentation of medals.

1982 Library Association involved in financial pruning: Youth Libraries Group takes more responsibility for medal.

1985 Secrecy reintroduced before announcement of medal.

1986 Fiftieth anniversary since medal first awarded.

APPENDIX B

Carnegie Medal Winners and Commended Books 1936–1984

1936   *Pigeon Post*: Arthur Ransome (Cape)
       Second *Sampson's Circus*: Howard Spring (Faber)
       Third *Ballet Shoes*: Noel Streatfeild (Dent)

1937   *The Family from One End Street*: Eve Garnett (Muller)

1938   *The Circus is Coming*: Noel Streatfeild (Dent)

1939   *The Radium Woman*: Eleanor Doorly (Heinemann)

1940   *Visitors from London*: Kitty Barne (Dent)

1941   *We Couldn't leave Dinah*: Mary Treadgold (Cape)

1942   *The Little Grey Men*: 'B.B.' (Eyre & Spottiswoode)

1943   Award withheld as no book considered suitable.

1944   *The Wind on the Moon*: Eric Linklater (Macmillan)

1945   Award withheld as no book considered suitable.

1946   *The Little White Horse*: Elizabeth Goudge (U.L.P.)

1947   *Collected Stories for Children*: Walter de la Mare (Faber)

1948   *Sea Change*: Richard Armstrong (Dent)

1949   *The Story of your Home*: Agnes Allen (Faber)

1950   *The Lark on the Wing*: Elfrida Vipont (O.U.P.)

1951   *The Wool-pack*: Cynthia Harnett (Methuen)

1952   *The Borrowers*: Mary Norton (Dent)

Appendix B

1953 *A Valley Grows Up*: Edward Osmond (O.U.P.)

1954 *Knight Crusader*: Ronald Welch (O.U.P.)
COMMENDED
The Children of Green Knowe: Lucy M. Boston (Faber)
Over the Hills to Fabylon: Nicholas Stuart Gray (O.U.P.)
The Horse and His Boy: C. S. Lewis (Bles)
The Lady of the Linden Tree: Barbara Leonie Picard (O.U.P.)
English Fables and Fairy Stories: James Reeves (O.U.P.)
The Eagle of the Ninth: Rosemary Sutcliff (O.U.P.)
Special Commendation
Lavender's Blue: Kathleen Lines (O.U.P.)

1955 *The Little Bookroom*: Eleanor Farjeon (O.U.P.)
COMMENDED
Man Must Measure: Lancelot Hogben (Rathbone)
Candidate for Fame: Margaret Jowett (O.U.P.)
The Story of Albert Schweitzer: Jo Manton (Methuen)
A Swarm in May: William Mayne (O.U.P.)
Minnow on the Say: Philippa Pearce (O.U.P.)

1956 *The Last Battle*: C. S. Lewis (Bodley Head)
COMMENDED
The Fairy Doll: Rumer Godden (Macmillan)
Chorister's Cake: William Mayne (O.U.P.)
The Member for the Marsh: William Mayne (O.U.P.)
Ransom for a Knight: Barbara Leonie Picard (O.U.P.)
The Silver Sword: Ian Serraillier (Cape)
The Shield Ring: Rosemary Sutcliff (O.U.P.)

1957 *A Grass Rope*: William Mayne (O.U.P.)
COMMENDED
The Warden's Niece: Gillian Avery (Collins)
Songbirds Grove: Anne Barrett (Collins)
Falconer's Lure: Antonia Forest (Faber)
The Blue Boat: William Mayne (O.U.P.)
The Story of the Second World War: Kathleen Savage (O.U.P.)
The Silver Branch: Rosemary Sutcliff (O.U.P.)

Appendix B

1958 *Tom's Midnight Garden*: Philippa Pearce (O.U.P.)
COMMENDED
The Chimneys of Green Knowe: Lucy M. Boston (Faber)
Warrior Scarlet: Rosemary Sutcliff (O.U.P.)

1959 *The Lantern Bearers*: Rosemary Sutcliff (O.U.P.)
COMMENDED
The Load of Unicorn: Cynthia Harnett (Methuen)
The Borrowers Afloat: Mary Norton (Dent)
The Rescuers: Marjorie Sharp (Collins)
Friday's Tunnel: John Verney (Collins)
Quiet as Moss: Andrew Young (Hart-Davis)

1960 *The Making of Man*: I.W. Cornwall (Phoenix House)
COMMENDED
The Great Gale: Hester Burton (O.U.P.)
The Penny Fiddle: Robert Graves (Cassell)
The Bonny Pit Laddie: Frederick Grice (O.U.P.)
Seraphina: Mary K. Harris (Faber)
The Ivory Horn: Ian Serraillier (O.U.P.)

1961 *A Stranger at Green Knowe*: Lucy M. Boston (Faber)
COMMENDED
Peter's Room: Antonia Forest (Faber)
Miss Happiness and Miss Flower: Rumer Godden (Macmillan)
Ragged Robin: James Reeves (Heinemann)
February's Road: John Verney (Collins)

1962 *The Twelve and the Genii*: Pauline Clarke (Faber)
COMMENDED
The Greatest Gresham: Gillian Avery (Collins)
Castors Away: Hester Burton (O.U.P.)
Armour and Blade: S. E. Ellacott (Abelard-Schuman)
The Summer Birds: Penelope Farmer (Chatto & Windus)
The Story of John Keats: Robert Gittings and Jo Manton (Methuen)
Windfall: K. M. Peyton (O.U.P.)

Appendix B

1963 *Time of Trial*: Hester Burton (O.U.P.)
   COMMENDED
   The Latchkey Children: Eric Allen (O.U.P.)
   Kings, Bishops, Knights and Pawns: Life in a Feudal Society: Ralph Arnold (Constable)
   Castaway Christmas: M. J. Baker (Methuen)
   The Thursday Kidnapping: Antonia Forest (Faber)
   Hell's Edge: John Rowe Townsend (Hutchinson)

1964 *Nordy Bank*: Sheena Porter (O.U.P.)
   COMMENDED
   London's River: Eric de Mare (Bodley Head)
   The Three Brothers of Ur: J. G. Fyson (O.U.P.)
   The Namesake: C. Walter Hodges (Bell)
   The Maplin Bird: K. M. Peyton (O.U.P.)

1965 *The Grange at High Force*: Philip Turner (O.U.P.)
   COMMENDED
   The Journey of the Eldest Son: J. G. Fyson (O.U.P.)
   Elidor: Alan Garner (Collins)
   The Bus Girls: Mary K. Harris (Faber)
   The Orchestra and Its Instruments: Christopher Headington (Bodley Head)
   The Plan for Birdmarsh: K. M. Peyton (O.U.P.)
   One is One: Barbara Leonie Picard (O.U.P.)

1966 Award withheld as no book considered suitable.
   Highly Commended
   The Bayeux Tapestry: The Story of the Norman Conquest: Norman Denny and Josephine Filmer-Sankey (Collins)
   COMMENDED
   The Wild Horse of Santander: Helen Griffiths (Hutchinson)
   Thunder in the Sky: K. M. Peyton (O.U.P.)
   Marassa and Midnight: Morna Stuart (Heinemann)

1967 *The Owl Service*: Alan Garner (Collins)
   Highly Commended
   The Dream Time: Henry Treece (Brockhampton)

Appendix B

COMMENDED
The Piemakers: Helen Cresswell (Faber)
Smith: Leon Garfield (Longman)
Flambards: K. M. Peyton (O.U.P.)

1968 *The Moon in the Cloud*: Rosemary Harris (Faber)
Honours list
The Whispering Mountain: Joan Aiken (Cape)
When Jays Fly to Barbmo: Margaret Balderson (O.U.P.)
Black Jack: Leon Garfield (Longman)

1969 *The Edge of the Cloud*: K. M. Peyton (O.U.P.)
Honours list
The Nightwatchmen: Helen Cresswell (Faber)
The Intruder: John Rowe Townsend (O.U.P.)

1970 *The God Beneath the Sea*: Edward Blishen and Leon Garfield (Longman)
Honours list
The Devil's Children: Peter Dickinson (Gollancz)
The Drummer Boy: Leon Garfield (Longman)
Ravensgill: William Mayne (Hamish Hamilton)

1971 *Josh*: Ivan Southall (Angus & Robertson)
Highly Commended
A Likely Lad: Gillian Avery (Collins)
Up the Pier: Helen Cresswell (Faber)
Tristan and Iseult: Rosemary Sutcliff (Bodley Head)

1972 *Watership Down*: Richard Adams (Rex Collings)
COMMENDED
The Dancing Bear: Peter Dickinson (Gollancz)
No Way of Telling: Emma Smith (Bodley Head)

1973 *The Ghost of Thomas Kempe*: Penelope Lively (Heinemann)
COMMENDED
Carrie's War: Nina Bawden (Gollancz)
The Dark is Rising: Susan Cooper (Chatto & Windus)
The Bongleweed: Helen Cresswell (Faber)

Appendix B

1974 *The Stronghold*: Mollie Hunter (Hamish Hamilton)
COMMENDED
The Battle of Gettysburg: Ian Ribbons (O.U.P.)

1975 *The Machine Gunners*: Robert Westall (Macmillan)
COMMENDED
The Grey King: Susan Cooper (Chatto & Windus)
Dogsbody: Diana Wynne Jones (Macmillan)

1976 *Thunder and Lightnings*: Jan Mark (Kestrel)
COMMENDED
The Blue Hawk: Peter Dickinson (Gollancz)

1977 *The Turbulent Term of Tyke Tiler*: Gene Kemp (Faber)
COMMENDED
Under Goliath: Peter Carter (O.U.P.)
A Charmed Life: Diana Wynne Jones (Macmillan)
The Shadow Cage: Philippa Pearce (Kestrel)

1978 *The Exeter Blitz*: David Rees (Hamish Hamilton)
COMMENDED
A Kind of Wild Justice: Bernard Ashley (O.U.P.)
The Battle of Bubble and Squeak: Philippa Pearce (Deutsch)
Devil on the Road: Robert Westall (Macmillan)

1979 *Tulku*: Peter Dickinson (Gollancz)
Highly Commended
The Castle Story: Sheila Sancha (Kestrel)
COMMENDED
Which Witch?: Eva Ibbotson (Macmillan)
The Vandal: Ann Schlee (Macmillan)

1980 *City of Gold*: Peter Dickinson (Gollancz)
Highly Commended
Nothing to be Afraid of: Jan Mark (Kestrel)
COMMENDED
The Fox in Winter: John Branfield (Gollancz)
A Sense of Shame: Jan Needle (Deutsch)

Appendix B

1981 *The Scarecrows*: Robert Westall (Macmillan)
   Highly Commended
   The Hollow Land: Jane Gardam (Julia MacRae)
   COMMENDED
   Bridget and William: Jane Gardam (Julia MacRae)
   Goodnight Mister Tom: Michelle Magorian (Kestrel)

1982 *The Haunting*: Margaret Mahy (Dent)
   Highly Commended
   The Dark Behind the Curtain: Gillian Cross (O.U.P.)
   COMMENDED
   Wall of Words: Tim Kennemore (Faber)

1983 *Handles*: Jan Mark (Kestrel)
   Highly Commended
   Talking in Whispers: James Watson (Gollancz)
   COMMENDED
   The Way to Sattin Shore: Philippa Pearce (Kestrel)
   A Little Fear: Patricia Wrightson (Hutchinson)

1984 *The Changeover*: Margaret Mahy (Dent)
   Highly Commended
   Brother in the Land: Robert Swindells (O.U.P.)

Index

Adams, Richard 19
Aiken, Joan 10, 20, 29
Alderson, Brian 8, 11, 23, 34
Allen, Mabel Esther 14
Ardizzone, Edward 23, 33
Ashley, Bernard 15
Avery, Gillian 20

Balderson, Margaret 29
Ballet Shoes 4
Barne, Kitty 18, 23, 32
Battle of Bubble and Squeak, The 36
Bawden, Nina 10
Betty Trask Award 37
The Blue Hawk 20
Bodley Head 35
Booker McConnell Prize 24, 34, 37
Bookseller, The 34
Borrowers, The 24–25
Boston, Lucy M. 39–40
Boyle, Edward 33
Bridget and William 28
Bronowski, Jacob 33
Brookner, Anita 37
Brother in the Land 23
Butler, Joan 28
Butterfly Ball, The 36

Carpenter, Humphrey 29
Causley, Charles 27
Cawley, Winifred 19
Chambers, Aidan 8, 21, 27
Chambers, Nancy 28
Charmed Life 20
Chosen for Children 10, 32–33
Circus is Coming, The 5
City of Gold 24
Collected Stories for Children 18
Colwell, Eileen 5–6, 8–10, 31, 32

Corbett, E. V. 7, 12
Corbett, W. J. 36
Cornwall, I. W. 26
Cresswell, Helen 11
Crouch, Marcus 10, 32–33

Daily Mirror 35
Davies, Andrew 19
de la Mare, Walter 18, 32, 33
Dent 18
Devil in the Fog 19
Dickinson, Peter 10, 20, 24, 36
Dohm, Janice 9
Doorly, Eleanor 6, 32
Dream Time, The 11

Edge of the Cloud, The 20
Eleanor Farjeon Award 11
Elidor 21–22
Elkin, Judith 42
Emperor's Winding Sheet, The 36

Family From One End Street, The 28
Farjeon, Eleanor 19
Federation of Children's Book Groups 14, 16
Financial Times 37
Fisher, Margery 8
Flambards 11
Fyson, J. G. 21

Gardam, Jane 28, 36
Gardner, Frank 20
Garfield, Leon 11, 19, 29, 35
Garner, Alan 10, 11, 21, 29–30
Garnett, Eve 28
Gaskell, Janet 25
Ghost of Thomas Kempe, The 37
God Beneath The Sea, The 24, 43

Index

Golding, William 26
Goodnight Mister Tom 19, 20
Graham, Eleanor 5, 31
Grange At High Force, The 21–22, 23
Greene, Graham 26
Griffiths, Vivien 24
Guardian Award 11, 13, 19–20

Handles 41
Harris, Rosemary 29
Hayler, Ethell 5
Heeks, Peggy 10, 11
Hildick, E. W. 8
Hill, Janet 9, 11, 12
Hoban, Russell 36
Hobbit, The 28–29
Hollow Land, The 28, 36
Hotel du Lac 37
How Tom Beat Captain Najork and his Hired Sportsmen 36
Hughes, Ted 27, 29

Iron Man, The 29

Jones, Diana Wynne 20
Jones, Harold 22–23
Journey of the Eldest Son 21–22
Junior Bookshelf 18
Junior Education 38

Kemp, Gene 23
King-Smith, Dick 28

Last Battle, The 19
Laura Ingalls Wilder Award 10
Lavender's Blue 22
Leeson, Robert 5, 18
Lewis, C. S. 19, 32, 33
Lewis, Naomi 8
Library Assistant 4
Library Association Record 4, 16, 18, 24, 31, 35
Likely Lad, A 20
Lines, Kathleen 22
Lively, Penelope 36, 37

MacDonald, Shelagh 36
McGough, Roger 27

Machine Gunners, The 16, 25
McVitty, Walter 23
Magorian, Michelle 19, 20
Mahy, Margaret 10
Making of Man, The 26
Mann, Andrew 23
Mark, Jan 10, 19, 40–41
Marquez, Gabriel Garcia 26
Mayne, William, 10, 22
Meek, Margaret 8
Memory in a House 39
Milne, A. A. 19
Moon in the Cloud, The 29
Murison, W. J. 24

National Book League 14
New York Herald Tribune Prize 29
Newbery Medal 3, 17, 25, 30, 36–37
Newbery Medal Books, 1922–1955 32
No End to Yesterday 36
Nobel Prize 26, 43
Nursery World 38

One is One 21–22
Osmond, Edward 32
Other Award 7, 13–14, 16, 23, 42
Owl Service, The 11, 20, 34
Oxford University Press 7, 18, 20–22

Parrott, Phyllis 32
Parsons, Ian 33
Paulin, Lorna 7
Pearce, Philippa 21, 22, 36
Peter Pan Award 28
Peyton, K. M. 11, 22
Picard, Barbara Leonie 21
Piemakers, The 11
Pigeon Post 4, 19

Radium Woman, The 6, 18
Ransome, Arthur 4, 18, 19, 31, 32
Ray, Sheila 42
Reluctant Reader, The 8, 21

Salway, Lance 25–26
Sampson's Circus 4
Sayers, W. C. Berwick 3, 4, 5, 27–28

Index

Schlee, Ann 20
Sheep Pig, The 28
Signal Poetry Award 27
Smarties Prize 28, 35, 37–38
Smith 11, 19
Song of Pentecost, The 36
Spring, Howard 4
Stevenson, Bruce 7, 11–12
Stitch in Time, A 36, 37
Stone Book Quartet 29–30
Stones, Rosemary 23
Stranger at Green Knowe, A 39
Streatfeild, Noel 4, 5, 18, 33
Sunday Times 35
Sutcliff, Rosemary 10, 21, 22
Swindells, Robert 23

Talking in Whispers 23
Times, The 34
Times Educational Supplement Information Book Award 27
Times Literary Supplement, The 8, 11
Tolkien, J. R. R. 28–29
Tom Fobble's Day 30
Tom's Midnight Garden 21, 25, 43

Townsend, John Rowe 10, 20, 29, 30
Treece, Henry 11
Tulku 36
Turbulent Term of Tyke Tiler, The 23, 30
Turner, Philip 21–22

Uttley, Alison 10

Vandal, The 20
Visitors from London 23

Walsh, Jill Paton 36
Warrior Scarlet 21
Watership Down 20, 24
Watson, James 23
Webb, Bill 20
Westall, Robert 10, 16, 19
When We Were Very Young 19
The Whispering Mountain 20
Whitbread Award 28, 34, 35–36
Whitbread, Samuel 35
Wood, Ken 24
Woodfield, H. J. B. 18

Your Guess Is As Good As Mine 15